THE
HEBDOMEROS SUITE
WITH THE
BRONZINO POEMS

Library and Archives Canada Cataloguing in Publication

Dault, Gary Michael
    The Hebdomeros suite and Bronzino poems / Gary Michael Dault.

ISBN 978-1-55096-251-2

    I. Art — Poetry. I. Title.

PS8557.A616H42 2011   C811'.54   C2011-907133-9

Design and Composition by Hourglass Angels–mc
Typeset in Birka at the Moons of Jupiter Studios
Printed by Imprimerie Gauvin

The publisher would like to acknowledge the financial assistance of
the Canada Council for the Arts and the Ontario Arts Council, which
is an agency of the Government of Ontario.

 Conseil des Arts du Canada **Canada Council for the Arts** 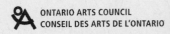 **ONTARIO ARTS COUNCIL** **CONSEIL DES ARTS DE L'ONTARIO**

Printed and Bound in Canada in 2011
Published by Exile Editions Ltd.
144483 Southgate Road 14 – GD
Holstein, Ontario, N0G 2A0 Canada

Sales / Distribution:
Independent Publishers Group
814 North Franklin Street, Chicago, IL 60610 USA
www.ipgbook.com   toll free: 1 800 888 4741

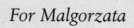

For Malgorzata

About Hebdomeros and about Bronzino

The Italian painter, Giorgio de Chirico, wrote *Hebdomeros*, his only novel, in 1929. Though undoubtedly one of the finest of a handful of memorable surrealist novels published around this time—André Breton's mysterious *Nadja*, for example, and Louis Aragon's intoxicating *Paris Peasant*—the work remained essentially unobtainable until it was republished in France in 1964. Poet John Ashbery produced the first English translation of *Hebdomeros* in 1992, and it is this text (published by Exact Change) I have respectfully if joyously plundered to forge the fifty poems making up my *Hebdomeros Suite*.

Perhaps it would be useful if I were to dilate a little upon this word "plundered." "Everything about *Hebdomeros*," writes Ashbery in his Introduction ("The Decline of the Verbs"), "is mysterious." And there was something so oddly open, so enterable, about de Chirico's swelling, oceanic prose-poetry, that it seemed not only permissible but actively desirable to take what I wanted from the painter's open-ended saga of his wandering metaphysician and generate my own Hebdomeros from my hit-and-run gleanings. In the end, there was very little of de Chirico's language left—scarcely anything. *Hebdomeros* was a word-hoard. I borrowed from it and then replaced almost everything I had borrowed with something new of my own.

It was the same with *The Bronzino Poems*. Here, my source was Deborah Parker's study, *Bronzino: Renaissance Painter as Poet* (Cambridge University Press, 2000). It was attractive to me that Bronzino (Agnolo di Cosimo, 1503-1572) was not only an exquisite painter but also a prolific and dashing writer—a maker of witty, passionate, brazen and wholly unforgettable sonnets. I grazed freely in the meadows of Parker's book, transforming what I liked best in Bronzino into new poems—which, as it turns out, are, not unexpectedly, mostly about being an artist and about making art.

Gary Michael Dault
Napanee, Ontario
September 29, 2011

THE HEBDOMEROS SUITE

Hebdomeros succeeds in this:

> yawning after his own bones
> eating the voices of birds
> bathing with swans

in all other endeavors

> he knows

how to settle his soul
at the other end of the table
and talk turkey

Spring arrived like a feather from a bird
settled in a bramble
                    schoolgirls came by
in their tiny waterfalls
rejoicing in the mending of the winter rent

Hebdomeros is a painter
              of violet evenings
other hues sometimes sit beside him
        but he returns always to violet
the *son et lumière* acropolis
slung round his neck
is pink in the morning
violet at night
        because he has conquered colour
with applications of pity

The air was balmy
the sky blue sea blue
the morning she came
in her murmuring
to see him
I believe I can find you, she cried
I believe I can see you
but she mistook him for an advance of cloud
a warm fogbank
and marched into the waves instead

Say a surface is convex in the middle
but flaccid and folded around the outside
like an apple pie
        terse enough to compromise the twilight
        but always in progress
        like a snowflake
        replaced by another snowflake
        equally fine
say the task fell to Hebdomeros
to open out the surface
and sleep on it under the moon
like a tame wolf

would he feel pity
for the realm of surfaces?
or would he sleep like a baby
in the arms of predictability?

The houses of Hebdomeros
are hidden behind bundles of oleander
witnesses to the harmonies of his inactivity
how perfectly clean is our town!
how free of the inexact refreshments
of the purposeful!
long live the heavy sighs
of Hebdomeros!

Hebdomeros
is said to be phrenologically thirsty
by which is meant
that he cares about amplitude
the give and take
set in motion by the pullulating mind
                    how he does go on
                    about surfaces!
he will tell you
                    for example
                                        whether or not
an afternoon has been flat or pitted
or if an evening seemed
smooth to the touch

The cities of Hebdomeros
        light the plane like candles
consequent in the night
        pebbles of flame
for a new landscape
        one sheet of paper
stands for a cloud
        one orange sits still
for the somnolent sun
        one branch gives off sparks
the horizon breaks into a sigh
        Hebdomeros smiles through his work
a blue jay winds his watch
        a cock drowns in an empty glass

I am profound
thought Hebdomeros
             in that
I have provoked my birth
with revelation after revelation
             the human crust has a certain value
and I have broken it through

Ah well
thought Hebdomeros
you have to think of

                  other things

but you mustn't use too bright a light

Mournful pedestrians
walking
in the cities of Hebdomeros
find their way blocked by sleep

they hold their children
by the hand
and tell them about their dreams
as the streetcars of Hebdomeros
rattle through the mists

Hebdomeros builds his cities
with straight lines
payed out with colonnades
there are no greetings
offered between pillars

A slight stomach ache
congruent with the stomach ache
you read about in the paper

a touch of indigestion you knew was coming
because the paper told you so
the burning was like a purchase

when the discomfort lifted
you felt it
following someone else's footsteps

your high spirits return
like flags on a windy day
unfurled until sundown

O starry night
o violincello
smoothing the waters
flooding over Hebdomeros' rushing heart
     making a wet garden
phosphorescent with moth and glow-worm
for settling his flowering blood
for pinching the flame
into a new comma of calm

Hebdomeros
distrusted originality
and was
therefore
mostly at home wherever he went

how dearly he loved
the pastoralism of the well-trodden
the unfinished state of mediocre cities

one day he spied a woman
with "under construction"
painted across her ass
                and fell in love
only to find later
that she had been completed earlier
despite her skirt's announcement

Hebdomoros lies in state
making lesser mortals wait
others live on rotten wood
he lives well on marble food
eating in the open air
in the quarry of his stare

The colour of morning
as the sun lifts its eyelids
is the colour
of Hebdomeros' eastern bedroom

in the evening
he tones it down to violet
puts the birds to bed
and turns his face to the west

You can't really leave
the middle of a room
or at least
Hebdomeros couldn't

he could walk to an edge
but that was still a middle
and if he walked back
the middle came at him like lightning

a point in space
is a place for an argument
and so thought Hebdomeros
if I never reach a point
there will be none

There are veils in the room
as fine and porous as sand
with perfumed guests beneath them
rigid like rulers
        the dining room is a wild sea
        asleep with the storm
tethered to Hebdomeros' finger
        he cracks the whip
        the room is pinched with thirst
the dinner guests are shipwrecked
        the chandeliers hang with dust

Hebdomeros walked forward slowly
and took two steps back
as if from a too easeful bargain

for he knows
the blue skies that fall upon serenities
crunched underfoot like fireworks
old carbon in the grass

oh for the lamps of autumn
thought Hebdomeros
and the wicks of poetry!

Hebdomeros
nourishes a broken column
in his garden
>
> its top is polished
> ready for the gliding of lizards
> he is hoping
> for the mysterious joy of ivy
>> there will be flowers at its foot

thought Hebdomeros
>> too tender for the column's beating wings
>> and marble beak
>> what flower can hold up its minor jewels
>> against the infinite stanzas of building?

Hebdomeros dotes
on the night's moths
the way they singe
their breathy wings
in the lamps
of his eyes
the way they brush his forehead
before dying
leaving the powder of their ideas
in his hair

One afternoon
Hebdomeros grew displeased
with the spectacle of
the agitated and mechanized cities
of which he had so far approved
deciding all of a sudden
to wash everything he had built
in lamplight
          a city
thought Hebdomeros
should be as clean and heavy as fresh milk
blue as a mussel
with buildings like needles

Hebdomeros caught a cold
his nose ran like lava
he drank midnight milk
and ate hard white strawberries
    he dragged himself
along the sand of all his cities
weeping like a wet crab
    on the last day of his cold
    he broke a branch of orange blossoms
    and held it aloft like a fasces
    at which time
    the cold left him

Every room Hebdomeros built
had a room with a ghost next door

the way layer after layer of silt
piles up on the ocean floor

it works to level the fallen guilt
it works to even the rising score

and he buried himself in his mother's quilt
and refused to say anything more

Hebdomeros loses all his keys
to the point where he cannot move
it means he's unable to leave his house
which leaves him nothing to prove

Quick said Hebdomeros
my bath is running
the oceans are opening
the rushing waters are as solemn
against the whiteness of the paper tub
as gulls are commas
beaked
in the discourse of clouds

the bath brimming,
a great sadness
drowned Hedomeros' heart
for as he settled himself
in the soft cup of his basin
he saw that he was becoming
progressively
post-hierarchical,
that there was nothing left but his toes
to issue command
how dry he felt in the slickness of the water
brittle
in the oily surge

Hebdomeros knew
the bath was the brother of sleep
and pulled the diamond plug

Hebdomeros
saw himself
as part of the night sky
as the stars
pointing out
the two-fisted deer-slayer
with arrows for hair
and a bow in his lengthy arm

the only other constellation
he could see
was the twinkling
Grotto of Dismal Palaces
where time's virtuous kings
lived and reigned
far along the universe's
cobbled road
      Hebdomeros asked nothing
      of the heavens
      but to stand still
      and open its door

All statues
of Hebdomeros
were pink
made of an absorptive marble
that kept the tincture of sunrise
long into the morning
and maintained the flush of sunset
far into the night

Hebdomeros
went for a walk in the dawn
past the promise of dark windows
sleeping cars parked
shivering with dew
stilled dogs
he felt he could see through the walls
to the tangled sleepers inside
arms thrown out like branches
breathing the coarse new light

Hebdomeros
was the driver, switch in hand,
of the beast of burden
that was him as well
                    and so each trip
                    was an ouroboros map
showing the pinprick man and master
riding each other
into the lathers of ongoing dawn
and the next gnashing twilight

The darkness
slid over Hebdomeros
scraping away
at the pores of his history
there was a scratch of lightning
long and straight like a dragonfly
a dishtowel moth
settled on his striated brow
like a powdered mask
the evening opened
its long-closed chambers
Hebdomeros settled into the night
cradled by the red eyes of earth

Hebdomeros tried to sleep
but the curtains rustled
into the room
and snapped their whips
until his bed danced
                he tried to think of his fiancée
                and her red fingernails
                which, when deployed,
                could brake the reeling
but the curtains sighed into a road
which Hebdomeros duly followed
                until
transparent with exhaustion
he came to the sun

Hebdomeros has banned noise
from all his cities:
     the buildings are rubber
     the streets are spongy
     the cars travel on beach balls
     the inconsiderate voice
speaking is punished as if it were onanism
     wording-off they call it
     words spilled on the ground
shouting by beheading
     birds who fly there by mistake
are regarded as gibbering demons

Every morning
Hebdomeros bought a night-shot bird
from his octogenarian hunter
which he did not eat
until the following evening
for he liked
in his moments of leisure
to paint
still lifes of game

        he would arrange
        the dead bird
        on the table
        with a napkin
        sometimes circling it
        with cotton batting
        as if it were snow
      which made him think of hunting again
and the need to purchase another bird
            at dinner hour
he plucked the bird himself
placed it in a pot
with some goat's butter and salt
turning it round with a fork
chanting
"It must feel the heat!
It must feel the heat!"
as it cooked

Hebdomeros
detested
ice cubes in his drink

he saw nothing
redeemed
by the silvery clink

the clash in the glass
never
helped him to think

The logs blazed
in Hebdomeros' fireplace
shadows laughed up the walls
a bowl of figs
resting on the hearth
caught fire
hissing syrup
and spangling the room
with sweet sweat of the fruit
Hebdomeros detested figs
almost as much
as he despised strawberries
and cream
he was happy
therefore
to watch the figs crinkle into cinders

Hebdomeros
felt that all movement
ought to be northward
even the shortest steps
trips to the grocer
bringing in the paper
you make the journey
however few feet you move
all the same we should go north
he would say to his companions,
his neighbours his children
the north, he would say
is a little like the west
pocketing the sun
and distributing sleep
whereas
the south is a little like the east
a place of deleterious
corrosive lands
where your bones
hang in an air as thin as shell
where your eyes sting
in scalding shadow

As he finished
his speech in the harbour
Hedomeros winked at his frigates
which curtseyed out into the bay:
the official fleet of Hebdomeros
trim as seagulls
puffed as water-lions
smiling out onto the doubtful ocean

"Hebdomeros fell silent
and stared thoughtfully
at the gentle arabesques
of an oriental carpet he had just bought"
he held out his eyes
to the purchasable tongues of flame
and knitted his brow
at the surge of knots
henceforward
said Hebdomeros
to nobody whatsoever
the streets of my cities
shall be woven like carpets
and the people
shall lie down where they are
and die when they like

He does not get angry
though sometimes he clutches
the arms of his chair
and his knuckles
grow white
        the feelings
        of his companions are thus spared
though all his furniture
is bruised
and dry

Luxurious foods
infamous nourishment
skirting the paths of the body
nourish little eventualists
who lie in the bones' bushes
at the bending of the joints
waiting to spring
      sometimes Hebdomeros
      overate
after which he could taste
the body's viewpoint:
           a wagon-wheel
           with burning rubbish
              at the hub

A box of chocolates
for Hebdomeros
sent from the townsfolk
to poison his afternoon

Hebdomeros chose a cherry
        and turned sugar-white
all the rest of the chocolates
kept their eyes on him
        will he won't he
join in the sweet round?
                to Hebdomeros
the chocolates looked like soldiers
in bunkers
                a chill fell over
the garden

the chocolates shivered in the box

Hebdomeros
tireless collector
        fired his ancient imprecise pistols
and made a collector's decision:
        he would push his boat
lightly from the shore
        and gather all the polished
stones lining his lambent beaches
        and did so,
lifting them by the shovelful
        from the seaweed sand
        until his boat sank
and the ocean lapped up the land

Hebdomeros
in his chapel
rarely there
on his knees
on a wide stone disc
at the foot of a shaft of light
like a pea on a plate

saw a clutch of visions
in the deep church night:
two bulky men
bent over him
with axes

One hot dislocated night
when parked cars
still burned your hand
at midnight
and the breath of peonies
came at you like gas
            Hebdomeros
decided on some ice cream
in the din of hot stars
that garlanded his simmering city
                but there were
so many flavours in the night:
mystic flavours, whereby the ice cream
            could be made to taste like chimes
or swallows piercing the sunrise
            or yellowing blades of grass
or even the blue wave of a moment's ennui,
that Hebdomeros' ice cream desire
            slowly melted against the morning
                and he decided on
            conditional tea
with a few slices of circumspect toast

One afternoon
deep in his garden
Hebdomeros decided
to be tranquil for a very long time
all flowers rustle
thought Hebdomeros
and retired to his library
where—little surprise!—he could
hear the pages of his books
moving like sandpaper
one upon another
                    generating dust

the world rolls over
like a dog
thought Hebdomeros
its people jump from its back
like fleas

Hebdomeros
toured his biggest factory
the day it shut down
     its jaws ceased to grind
     its rotors rolled slowly to a point
beads of oil seeped onto the floor beneath the grinders
the pressure dropped to darkness

nothing left but poetry
     thought Hebdomeros
        kicking off his steel-toed boots
     and turning in his goggles
to follow
         the sweep of a dusty falcon
lifting from the roof
     screaming   across the scrim of ashen sky

Hebdomeros
sat high on the trunk of a broken column
pondering the weight of the state
and the state of weighty things
     his hand resting
gently on his shoulder
     suddenly
          his voice started up
like a thrush from the underbrush
     chased into flight
       his eye was filled with words
a pincushion cloud pricked with language
       until a single hummingbird
its wings a sphere of beaten air
     came to trade his sparkling tirade
for a little peace and quiet
Hebdomeros climbed down
     from his fluted column

          a broken man

Deciding he had to flee
Hebdomeros plied his room
in a glass boat,
forced into the corners
at every turn
by the cubist undercurrent
that tugged at the sine-waves of his stern
teaching him fatal angles
                    at last abandoning
                    the crystal craft
and gathering all his clockwork strength
he hoisted himself
onto a high windowsill
fastened to the moldings like a spider
and gazed out to sea
and marvelled at all the true boats

I believe I can see it
said Hebdomeros
in the soft, ruminative version
of his tyrannical voice,
his telescope in reverse
the town which has no equal
lives in late afternoons
in the lapping heat
its marble quays
reach out like fingers
grasping at the boats of the world.
    I shall sail always
towards the town of my desire
rejecting the incommensurable weakness
of people with other opinions
    I shall find my town
before the gazelle of one more evening
dies fruitlessly
along the my heart's processional
     and lowering the blinds
Hebdomeros
lost himself in his chair

THE BRONZINO POEMS

To my extraordinary friends:
stone, water, mobs along the way
mops for the gritty heart
sticks and needles for attention

The countess stood in a puddle
her feet took root
feeding pure suspension
to her diadem brain

I took the chalk
my tubes of colour
lifted her signification
to peer under her marble skirts
and get down to work

My painting was a feather
in the afternoon sun
a crumb of dust
in her tablecloth eye

Onion enters at the eye
figs in memory
the colours of cream
crowded at the door like cats

Spend them at the easel
coins of the hand
and the fragrant palm
figs for brushes
onions for honour

Eleanora on a violin
repeats her needs
repeats her shame
her canine face her canine cap
her violin half smiling
her smile sodomitical
and still beguiling

I pressed my eyelids
and saw blue
exclamation points
on the yellow wall

gowns
on an armature
of lady bone
with its silver eyes

Verses of table and chairs
buttocks and eyelashes
appendages
you can sit on or next to
gazing upon the fruited spandrels
the juice of architecture
stinging for your eyes
        such ludic verses
I am unable to praise
and unable to prevent
yes I see them silting up
the burdened world
o for the simple hours
of Petrarch's bird

The painting floats
away beneath your feet
because I have affixed
to your silken shoulders
two flamingos
which you are now afraid
to look down and see

I invite the Arno to join me
to weep every morning

But rivers add their tears
only to the flow of innuendo
that slips by my lengthening wit
and will not grieve with me

and so I return to painting
crushed by division

Should I increase
or diminish
the world's complacent spaces
with my insinuating brush?

It amuses me
to feel richer than pigment
with the forest around me
the trees with their crooked fingers

che selva e questa?
It is never as inappropriate
as one wanted it to be

Venus and Cupid
like two keys on the piano
two teeth in a smile
two bubbles in a crowd of sharp edges

Cupid the dwarf
Venus-bird in its hand
an owl on its head
a flashlight in its mouth
four daggers

I'll give them
the whir
of cellophane wings

He made one wing white
and the second wing red

which sharpened the eye
and streamlined the head

the angel spun round
in prismatic disgrace

while the painter grew rich
from the egg on his face

Take a breath from the sails
and a course from the snails
a tattered break in the moon
gravity fed by a spoon

Now to paint
the best bending surface
that ever graced a fat mirror
or a countess's molecular ass

Two potent wills in congruence:
my left hand and my right
underemployed by undertow
contrition to be set right

Pastoralism of the old school:
a walk in a stony field
disinterring concrete sheep
painting the meadow's yield

One effulgent night
I was arrested
for reaching up
unscrewing stars in their sockets
one by one
until Florence was black as legality

I got out of jail fast enough
if you're going to get drunk
it's safer to wear a dress suit*

*e.e. cummings, quoted by John Dos Passos in *The Best Times*. New York: Signet Books, 1966, p. 151.

There are snow-tipped mountains
at the end of my studio
with vitaminized clouds
that catch me when I fall upwards

There are forces
that are a type of law
and weaknesses
that get the job done
they curve
about the hub of my heart
like leopards on hot rocks

In middle age
my voice grew disproportionately loud
I could bring down a cathedral
with a cough
or start an avalanche
by clearing my throat

women dissolved
when I talked to them
children sifted into sugar

there were only mountains
to talk to

Eleanora put the veil aside
and spoke like a woman
thinned by immodesty

her voice was a cut lawn
little unused thoughts to one side
browning at my attentions

her talk was like a highway
with a toll booth

When I wake up
too far away from awe

I make destitute pilgrimages
to available light *

a bronze bell
a fireplace
or a struck match

* "Cette flamme dont j'avais besoin, une bougie me la preta, mobile
comme le regard" [*This flame I needed, a candle lent it me, mobile like the
gaze*], from René Char, *Arsenal*, quoted in Mary Ann Caws, *A Metapoetics
of the Passage*. London: University Press of New England, 1981, p. 79.

Here's a little root
which, when eaten
will give you wings*

and so I ate
from the bitter stalk
falling down with the porous bite

caught by a third register of space
which I do not call
flying

* Aristophanes, *The Birds,* translated by Benjamin Bickley Rogers (New York: Doubleday Anchor Books, 1955), p. 38.

Gravity
predicates the tear
rounds the eyebrow
deep-falls the gown
creating invitation

Brevity
puts it all back
puffing the soul's balloon
rounding its sides
holding onto the handles
of levitation

make the nude
sheer as a tear
sonnet-tight
with the brace
of a cold wind

then you can prop her
in a gallery
a salt-block nude
for a pasture with cows

I have walked
bare crumbly hills
wearing the cap of a dog

whatever it takes
to tamp down
the surfaces of things

I have walked away
backwards
believing in the she-truths*
that mute a man's horn

I have been on the level
like a lake

<hr />

* "She-truths" is from Edward Dahlberg, *The Flea of Sodom*. New York:
Direction 18, 1955, p. 53.

I speak the language of the sea
and also of the brush
which rasps into the sea

your breasts
rise among the swells
my eyes swim to your side
like more nipples

the distant shores
smoke like vestments
we walk together
towards the befuddled dawn

There are underclothing people
who want to be artists
whose pinions tremble
at the undercutting of a jar
or the belch of a fat vase

They try everything:
bruised nettles
on their genitalia
thistles and scorpions
in their art-fat armpits

Nothing serves.
I suggest
a poultice of pigment
wherever it hurt
and a peck of lupines*
for after the sting

* "a peck of lupines" is Dahlberg, *op.cit.*, p. 65

Bronzino caught a cold
which bit his flesh with softened teeth
and reduced him to oily tears

Is this the street's moisture
or my Eleanora's breath
come to visit me as fog?
he asked

All day Bronzino held bravely to his bed
refusing to leave
the snowy fields of his clarity
for anything short of a steamy piss

At night
he grew unaccountably restless
fearing the darkness would die in his mouth
empty the bottles of his eyes

He most distrusts
the daily nothings
the way the newspaper
hits the porch
or the way a philodendron
grows an inch
when you look away
these small pushes
against his pelvic clock
drive the liquid from his bones
he longs for mermaids
instead of for women

Bronzino
mistaking her eyelids
for petals*
painted her
as a blue bouquet

and fell to weeping
at the loss of his home

*see Apollinaire's "Mai" from his *Rhenish* poems ("...Les petales tombées
des cerisiers de mai / Sont les ongles de celle que j'ai aimée / Les petales
fletries sont comme ses paupières...."). Caws, *op.cit.*, p. 92.

Oh Bronzino!
poor, self-pitying plague!
you began as an optical empire
leaning on the arms of armless girls
and now
poisoned by paradox
you slant into the salons
of those rich enough to starve you
and poor enough
to bloat you like a bladder

Why don't you learn
from stray cats
you fangless frog?
And isn't there something to be gleaned
from the cats who hurl themselves
into the Arno every night
to flee the pull of the pillow?

Back on the road
riding a painterly mule
ears and tail for brushes
honking yawp
for whining and whelking
Bronzino took his studio
travelling
sometimes stopping
to paint girls
labouring in the fields
and resting by the roadside
trotting along
sketching the narrative unfold
tree by tree
breast by breast

Bronzino shut his eyes for a moment
when he opened them again
his lands were cut-glass and milk
a giant diadem of edge and angle

Disgusted
he pulled off his boots of cloud
and closed his agate door

Two self-adjusting blues
trimmer than water
alighted on his shoulders

Two yellows
stared him in the face
one of corn one of hair

Two smoking reds
lit his cigar
and stuck it into the ground
where it grew into a cherry tree
with smoking fruit

Bronzino settled into the back seat
like a bone in a dish

An evening
sky of parasols
opened over the car

Take me to the lion's roar
he told the driver

I am painting her arm
white as the bone
beneath her flesh

I am painting her dress
white as the flesh
that drapes the bone

I am painting her breath
white as the sleeping ghost
curled in her heart
that she thinks of as a soul

The short shadows
at the end
of a long haughty afternoon
give me a whole new people
to grow upon

I am building the chance
within my armistice heart
that my dry monsoon
will gutter and fibrillate
as I cast my weaknesses
in bronze

Your eyes freeze me solid
now I can get down to work

Wherever I look
the distance lights up like dawn
while closer to home
at the end of my arm
a nightingale
sings an amber darkness
full-throated as sherry

The brushes in my hand
turn into trees
and bloom in the dichotomous air

And so I paint
the fronts and backs of things
their lengths and shortness
heat on one side
cold on another:
the battery of art

My subject is
naked with pigment

she shines from linseed oil
she looks like a basted duck
roasting

when she is done
I am done
and we will walk together
from the studio
like a couple after dinner

Today is New Year's Day
I turn cartwheels of meditation
in the courtyard
for no good idea ever came to me
in stillness

I have decided
to mix
the penitential tears
of my aching,
too-long-posed models
into my pigments,
where their prismatic exhaustion
can attenuate each hue
and round each brushstroke
into a pillar of salt

I pulled a woman from the sand
she was made of china
she whispered to me of forsakenness
I stood her
in the middle of a meadow
where she sang
of the solitary mind of the sun
which had baked her brittle

I pulled a woman from the sea
she was made of phosphorous
she told me about watery darkness
I stood her
on dry land
where, in a voice flaked with silver,
she wailed to the moon
accusing it
of remorseless tidings

No ferment
bolts my hours

circles and arcs
rasp at my feet like dogs

a rose, a tomato
lodged in the corner of each eye

bones of black blood
pile up in the hallway
dropped
at the end of a beaten path

my brushes bend like grasses
purr like silkworms
how I hate them

Hurt by
the connection today
between beginning
with a freedom as lengthy as rope
and tomorrow
when someone will take lapidary scissors
to my frothy extensions
and cut me into unsuitable lengths

Listen gentlemen
with your telephone voices
scratching over the miles
between us
I am going to leave you all
the way the new body pulls away
from old slackening skin
I'll be your serpent
you can be my janitors

I am at the train station
but wary of boarding
lest being part of a train
I should be less of myself

I swim steady like a shark
keep going
not to sink to the bottom

I fly like a Bird of Paradise
who cannot land
and must sleep in air

Critical answers to paintings
written in pink ink
like grapefruit juice
on the belly of a sow
in the gallery farmyard

responses
torn like tree roots
from the somnolent earth
all to wipe down a painting
while it's wet and cocky

I'd like to live in a tent
and keep a camel
paint with a walking stick
chew grass

No more dialogues
under the tree of life
apples and chesnuts to eat
picked up in the meadow

I can sleep through anything
but the night
war for example
or an argument in the street outside

The night folds back and forth
and I am alive
in the city of the morning
in the lacings of sun

The night in tatters
a vestment
thrown onto the floor
to be washed